Abby B. Longstreet

Good Form

Manners Good and Bad, at Home and in Society

Abby B. Longstreet

Good Form
Manners Good and Bad, at Home and in Society

ISBN/EAN: 9783337405175

Printed in Europe, USA, Canada, Australia, Japan

Cover: Foto ©Suzi / pixelio.de

More available books at **www.hansebooks.com**

GOOD FORM

MANNERS

GOOD AND BAD, AT HOME AND IN SOCIETY

WITH REMARKS UPON THE VALUE OF
TACT, COURTESY, AND CONVENTIONALITY

BY THE AUTHOR OF "CARDS: THEIR SIGNIFICANCE AND
PROPER USES," "DINNERS," "SOCIAL ETIQUETTE
OF NEW YORK," ETC.

FREDERICK A. STOKES COMPANY
MDCCCXC

CONTENTS.

GOOD MANNERS

MANNER AND MANNERS.

" THE more manner the less manners," is a statement entitled to our consideration. A man of high breeding does not emphasize the fact that he has enjoyed exceptional advantages or position. On the contrary, he simply follows the codified laws, or usages of the best society, neither exceeding nor slighting them.

Carlyle, that rebel against all littleness, spoke for all mankind when he said, " Good-breeding differs, if at all, from high breeding only as it gracefully remembers the rights of others, rather than gracefully insists upon its own rights." Of course Carlyle had his own countrymen and countrywomen in mind, but we are not wholly without class distinctions, and we can understand and benefit by his definition.

Could the world have been made to believe that truest of all truths, that there can be no higher or nobler rank than that of gentleman and gentlewoman, this little volume would be wholly needless. Birth and fortune do not make a race of " gentle-folk "

although inherited tendencies, the constant examples
of perfect speech and manners, with the leisure for
cultivation that money provides, have a wonderfully
beneficial effect; nor do scholastic acquirements of
themselves or even genius always produce this result.
Men and women of mediocre talents and accomplish-
ments are agreeable, even charming, when they are
courteous of speech, have polished manners, and are
unselfish and considerate.

Perfect conduct and speech are naturally expected
of the educated—the learned. There is no gift and
no acquirement that man or woman can have,
that is more admired and valued than learning, or
which carries greater weight and influence when accom-
panied by fine breeding and elegant, or as our elders
called them,—" courtly manners."

A fine address opens doors that are closed to
wealth, fame and beauty; "the charm of sweet courtesy" keeps them ajar. "Practice is everything,"
admitted a famous courtier whose manners in public
were perfect, although he never had any real consideration for others, as the tragedy in his family life showed
to an astounded world. His was the unpardonable,
and too common custom of being delicate and well-
mannered abroad, while coarse and careless in his
habits at home.

MANNERS AT HOME.

SALUTATIONS in the home circle, as well as the manner of receiving these, are as invariably cordial and habitual with a well-bred family as they would be if a guest were present, or one was entering or leaving a circle of new acquaintances. The practice of an invariable courtesy cultivates kindliness and produces a graciousness of facial expression. That need not, and should not be, however, a smile at all times. A habit of making pleasant inquiries is a great help in establishing an ease of manner, a tranquil self-forgetfulness that prevents timidity even when in the presence of the most illustrious persons. Timidity is nothing except self-remembrance, and self-remembrance is a subtle and mischievous form of selfishness. But good manners banish a dread of awkwardness and self-consciousness, and make life in society like a tune that sings in the memory and cannot be forgotten. The child may be taught fine-breeding when he learns to talk, when he studies his letters in his primer, or even with his prayers that should include the well-being of others with petitions for himself. This sweet spirit of doing as one would be done by is the foundation, and indeed it is the completed structure of good manners.

To rise when an older person—a superior—an invalid—a stranger, or an unfortunate social equal enters or leaves a room or house, is a graceful compliment always and a rigorous law for men in society whenever social equals are gathered in a group that is small enough for each one to be conscious of the presence of all the others. A young woman, in the same way, should rise whenever one who is matronly comes in or takes leave of the family circle. This is also good manners in a small group in society.

She is a selfish, underbred woman, if she be not unmistakably elderly, who anywhere takes the most comfortable, or most conspicuous seat in the room. If it is urged upon her, she may occupy it for a little while, but she should resign it quietly as soon as another woman enters, unless the latter is very young. This rule respecting easy chairs, or advantageous positions by the fire or the lamp, and rising when another one enters a family circle, is a law that does not apply to parents as regards their children, but is an exacting one for children towards their parents; also with others who are their elders. Especially should well-bred boys relinquish the best places to their sisters without suggestion, a concession that equally well-bred girls will not forget to acknowledge with as fine a courtesy of speech as they would if their brothers were guests in the house. Brothers, especially young men, who are invariably attentive and winning in their manner toward their sisters, commend themselves more to ladies by so doing, than by any other social grace.

It is a beautiful custom with many polished gentlemen to treat their sisters and their grown daughters with as gallant attention, and with as delicate a manner, as they could offer to the most honored guest or to a hostess at entertainments.

The effect of this charming respectfulness to a daughter or to a sister, is manifold. The girl has a fine standard of manner and character always before her. Her home has the elegance of high breeding, no matter how simple its *entourage*. She has also the best and most trustworthy of formulas by which to measure the gifts and graces of young men who may be interested in her. This devoted attention nourishes and maintains an affectionate respect, and inspires confidence between a father and his child. His attentive manner toward her mother, who is, of course, always considered first, and who receives the first courtesies, becomes the exacting measure by which she weighs and judges the young men whom she meets, and through a familiarity with the finest breeding, she learns what and whom to avoid in society.

It is not good manners for the gentlemen of a family to fail to offer seats to the ladies at table, whenever it is possible, or a guest has not anticipated them in this courtesy. There are households in which the chair of the hostess of the house is placed by a servant, but this is not the most refined or considerate custom, nor is it the best lesson for growing lads. The politeness or duty of a servant to a mother, sister or guest, has not the same charm and significance as attentions bestowed by those who are of the family.

A story of distress, an unpleasant allusion, a discussion of subjects upon which there are, or may be, serious differences of opinion, are improper topics for table talk. Religious beliefs and political opinions are never mentioned at the tables of well-bred persons where guests are present, nor at any time if disturbing beliefs are likely to be called forth. Scandal is not repeated in the family at any time, and except for unavoidable reasons, not at all.

The family do not take seats until the presiding lady is placed, except under pressure of unusual circumstances. No one leaves the board until all are ready to rise, unless it is necessary, and then not until a request to be excused has been made to the presiding woman, after which a general pardon for breaking the circle is asked of those assembled on rising. [For table usages, see " Good Form, in Dinners."]

It is indelicate to cough at table. One can almost always prevent it by a swallow of liquid, or a determined application of will. Sneezing may be avoided by pressing the finger upon the upper lips, close to the cartilage that separates the nostrils. If it is necessary to place a finger in the mouth, this graceless act is concealed by a napkin held by the other hand.

It is bad manners to put any one in the family to inconvenience through a lack of promptness in keeping an appointment or promise, or to show discomfort or annoyance, if one has been the sufferer from such an occurrence, when it was not easily avoidable. The fine-fibred person suffers more keenly when he or she is the cause of inconvenience to another, than can the person whom the mistake or misfortune has discommoded.

It is true courtesy to give as little pain as possible, but social and domestic exigencies are such that it cannot always be avoided. The kindly and graceful never forget to ask pardon for an inadvertence, a blunder or a mistake, no matter how trivial it is, nor upon how insignificant a person it fell. Even children suffer less hurt when an apology is made to them or forgiveness is asked for discommoding them. If a fine manner is expected of them when they are grown, it should be extended to them while they are still lads and lassies. What a child receives in youth, it seldom fails to return at maturity. It is high bred to bestow as much benefit and pleasure as one is able to command, and there are always the little courtesies,—*les pêtites morales* of daily life—within touch of each member of a household. Good manners in the household are like oil upon complicated machinery—like cushions spread over rough and wounding ways—but they are more im-

portant than anything else in their strong influence
upon character. The result of a refined early life
shows itself in all that a man or woman becomes.

An orderly mind does not accompany disorderly
conduct at home or in society. A scholar may be a
recluse, and because he is solitary in his life he may
not be acquainted with the ceremonies by which order-
liness is maintained among people; but he is not
beyond a sympathetic touch with the world when he
ventures into it. He may be awkward but he cannot
be coarse; he may be ungraceful but he is not discourteous. If he could add to his acquirements a
knowledge of the easy and polite manners of polished
people, his talents would be less obscured to those
who would gratefully benefit by them. "Manners
make the man," is a proverb honored for its antiquity,
but more for its truth.

THE USES OF CONVENTIONALITY.

DOUBTLESS the best definition of conventionality in its true sense is indicated in Goldsmith's epigram on Garrick:

> "Our Garrick's a salad; for in him we see,
> Oil, vinegar, sugar and salt agree."

Oil is essential for the smoothing of humanity's ways and means; sugar is indispensable for the sweetening of bitter things; vinegar is at once a preservative and an appetizer, and salt gives savor. Of conventionality, it may not inaptly be said, that it is the salt of society; but if the salt shall have lost its savor, wherewithal shall it be salted?

Conventionality means simply a codification of the highest contemporary customs. It is on its face, arbitrary. Many of its commands are apparently either stupid or capricious. Its most rigorous votaries are looked upon by the thoughtless as fashionable triflers. Those who defy its rules and offend against its prescriptions are foolishly applauded as original and self-respecting. But when examined carefully, the conventional codes

13

of every civilized country, differing as they do, in consequence of climate and other physical conditions, as well as religious usages and traditions, will be found to be a philosophical expression of the most refined social economy.

Conventionality is the national and international system of personal intercourse, which enables each individual to get the highest good and the greatest pleasure out of life. Its first aim is to preserve seclusion and maintain self-respect. Its second is to effect a suave reciprocity, by which the simple and benign canon, "Do as you would be done by," is made at once practicable, ceremonious and safe.

The foundation of true conventionality is gentleness. The world, from the time it began to think, set its seal upon this test of fine breeding. As religion teaches men how to die, conventionality teaches them how to live. It deals with small things as well as great. It is mightiest in the mighty, and it becomes kings better than their crowns. Etymologically it should mean mercy, for though Shakespeare puts the word in Portia's mouth in quite another sense, in the French, it retains its first significance, that of thanks for courtesy.

Every people have their own etiquette. But certain phases of development are to be noted in the evolutions of all social codes. For example, the earliest salutations were a prostration of the body before the person for whom the mark of homage was intended.

In the profoundly religious East, this custom still pre-
vails in the temples. In the courts of Oriental despot-
ism sovereignty also claims this mark of respect,
the ancient identification of Deity and monarch being
thus perpetuated. As civilization came westward,
certain abstractions ceased to be vital. In the West,
the individual not only does not prostrate himself ab-
solutely, but he holds himself erect, his salutation con-
sisting of a graceful curve of but one-half the body.
That is, the idea of personal dignity is never lost sight
of in the West.

Within obvious limits, conventionality is arbitrary,
is capricious, but it is never without some reason.
Those of its laws that seem ridiculous have outlived
the cause for their existence, and will disappear in
time. As soon as the artists of Japan began carica-
turing their ancient gods, the people began to realize
the humor of many of their myths; and forthwith not
only cast the effigies of the gods out of their homes,
but smiled away social traditions and hereditary
superstitions that had held sway for centuries.

There must always be a certain transitoriness in
merely social etiquette. What an Elizabeth demanded
a Victoria would not tolerate. The gallantry shown
to Martha Washington to-day would be a caricature of
respect. The phraseology that Benjamin Franklin
employed in addressing ladies of high degree would, if
now used, be proof of an unsettled mind. But in
every age the essence of conventionality remains un-

changeable; it is gentleness with a certain timely
ceremony; it is only the inessentials, the incidentals
that change.

Conventionality exacts of every individual only what
is due to his fellows. Whoever would be fair to those
around him must become familiar with its require-
ments and he must practise them invariably, except in
cases that only prove the necessity of its exactions.
Rebellion against conventionality may be the privilege
of genius or the resource of irresponsibility, but genius
has always paid a penalty of chagrin for such a course
and irresponsibility can expect nothing but social
ostracism which will surely be administered in good
time.

Conventionality stands barrier-fashion, between the
reserved and refined, and those who have not yet fit-
ted or adjusted themselves to the speech and manners
of well-bred persons. If those who comprehend its use
and significance object to its applications, it is apt to
be because it stands between them and a coveted recognition or association. To satisfy their pique they
berate conventionality, and declare its spirit to be
chilling and heartless.

Has a law ever been enacted, whether written or un-
written, that did not or does not oppress somebody?
Law makers reply, " Not one ! "

Happily the statutes of conventionality have a far
larger number of permissions than commands, and it
is when they give more pain than benefits to others,

that gentlewomen find gracious ways and means for being less than strictly conventional. To use formalities without wounding others is a trustworthy testimony of gentle breeding. Conventionality being a law of kindly speech and courteous manners, it is inexorably unforgiving to such as disobey it. No delicate-minded woman will entrench herself in its strong places from which she may send shafts of unjust or unkind social discriminations. Evil speaking its codes strictly forbid. It goes farther. It allows, perhaps it is not asserting too much to say that conventionality commands, the honorable woman to rebuke the dishonorable tongue by her manner, and if she be venerable enough in years, by her speech also.

For example, a little girl long years ago entered the room of a grand old gentlewoman—a patrician American, to ask a hurried question. She sat in an old-fashioned, stately chair. Against the soberly rich colors of its tall back, her handsome head was beautifully and appropriately framed. The soft white lace of her frilled cap took away none of the dignity of her high-bred face that remains in memory, the most revered of pictures. The gentle stir of her fine, small white hands did not discompose the sweet gravity of her posture, as her glittering knitting needles clicked from loop to loop of the stocking of the waiting and listening girl. Yet there was that in her attitude and deep composure that indicated much suppressed emotion. Her head was slightly bent over her work,

2

while a chattering woman, who had intruded into what
we children called "The presence," was relating in
wearisome and unpleasant detail an amazing and uncomplimentary story of a neighbor who had hitherto
borne an honorable name.

The little girl paused, knowing by much teaching
that well-bred children do not interrupt the speech of
their elders, and while thus waiting, not too pa-
tiently, she learned one of the most impressive and
influencing lessons of her youth.

The tale of the eager gossip was concluded—at
least she paused—perhaps only to take breath and go
on again with a morsel that seemed to be sweet to her.
The noble listener slowly folded her hands over the
knitting and lifting her head, looked steadily and
tranquilly into the face of her visitor. Her eyes had
in them the light of sorrowful indignation and severe
rebuke, when she broke her continued silence by saying with an impressive deliberation:

"Your story sounds like a falsehood. It ought to
be one. I shall treat it as such. Good-day and good-
bye."

The tale-bearer rose and paused, as if trying to understand what was meant, and then, dazed and
abashed, replied: "Good-day. I am sorry to have
displeased you."

This little event had its effect on the girl who wit-
nessed it for years, and is related here as an illustra-
tion of the value there may be in the uses of conven-

tionality in speech. It may silence lips that permit themselves an unkind liberty, or are eagerly critical of the blunders of their acquaintances, and alas! also those of their friends.

Of course there is another aspect of its last valuation that even excellent women have differed about. A repeated conversation will make clear what this difference of estimates may be. One woman said to another in a New York drawing-room: "Will you not allow me to propose your name for membership in 'The Kindly Club?'"

"Pray, what is 'The Kindly Club?'"

"To become a member of it a woman must promise never to speak in an unkind or uncomplimentary manner of another. That is all."

"All! Indeed, I shall do nothing of the sort. It would be base ingratitude. The club is not progressive; the best and highest characteristics I have attained are the results of uncomplimentary criticisms —judgments of me that in the main were fair and just. Through disapprovals by self-elected censors I learned the inferiority of my standards, and at once I strove to better them. No. I refuse to join 'The Kindly Club.'"

All have read of men who wore hair shirts and peas in their shoes and suffered other voluntarily applied afflictions in the hope and expectation of attaining righteousness. They may have been wise. We cannot know. But to rise to higher mental, moral or social levels through ill-natured gossip must be very much more torturing to delicate-minded women than to wear peas in their slippers.

MANNERS IN SOCIETY.

INDIVIDUAL characteristics are powerless to change in any perceptible manner the key note upon which civilized people have pitched the harmonies of what is known as society. Its composition is only varied by the slow movement of enlightenment. Its spirit is not lost among the multitude, because its *motif* is and always has been good will, and only by adhering to its formalities can one thoroughly enjoy his surroundings, unless he expects to live the life of a recluse. One may by gifted with adaptability and fall easily and quickly into the most graceful and charming of the prescribed ways of society. Others are born into them and know no other modes of social intercourse. Others there are who seem to have been born out of step with society. For these many things are difficult, but nothing that the world demands of them is impossible of acquirement. Such persons are apt to be misjudged by the superficial observer, but never by such as have studied human nature from a high social point of view.

It is not insincerity, much less is it a stupid affec-
tation, that often gives an unusual tone of voice, an
uncommon selection of words, or a stilted, unnat-
ural manner to certain respected persons, while they
are addressing strangers, but an unsettled and pain-
ful condition of mind which is pathetic and should be
cured. One element in it is self-consciousness, with
an eager desire to make a pleasant impression, which
ambition is by no means unworthy of the best of men
and women. It may also be due to an involuntary
reserve and delicacy which makes some men diffident
and causes them to conceal their real selves except
from friends.

On the other hand, it is often with the silly hope of
appearing to be of finer fibre than is natural or
desired, that the vain man and woman assume a
manner which they imagine is elegant, but observant;
well-bred persons seldom mistake the second for the
first class. Nor are they, if generous, without regret
that the first class should not so train their voices and
so perfectly acquire the habit of correct speech that
they need never risk misrepresenting themselves when
face to face with unfamiliar society. The last mentioned persons are seldom, if ever, aware that for them,
unfortunately, there are no kindly judgments and
little or no pity.

" Since you are able to conduct yourself so nearly
like a respectable man, why do you not study the arts
and graces of good manners, in order to practise them

habitually?" inquired Emerson of a person who for a brief season was tolerably civil.

Ah! and "why not?" may be also asked of the awkward, the discourteous and also of that most hopeless of all persons, the self-satisfied, upon whom company manners sit uneasily.

It is indecorous to be obstinate in little matters of form. George Washington allowed no one to be better-mannered than himself. His civil greeting and demeanor to the least important man or woman was as polished and as kindly as to persons of the highest rank. The gentleman always lifts or touches his hat to his acquaintances, whether men or women. The under-bred man may possibly lift his to a woman who is greatly his social superior, but not to his queal and never to his mother, wife, sister or to another man, and this expression of courtesy, is so easy and so graceful.

It is no longer good form to invite a young woman to drive, to go to any place of amusement, or indeed anywhere without first asking permission of her chaperone and then inviting both, provided the elder person accepts for her daughter or protégée. The chaperone is allowed to suggest an agreeable substitute for herself if she is engaged or is disinclined to be of service to the young people.

This recent innovation in American etiquette has been the most disagreeable of any social rule that has been adopted from foreign usages. Its wisdom is recognized by those who suffer most by its exactions, the chaperones of society. These women are the real martyrs, living over again, as they must, a life with which they were long ago satiated, smiling in the face of all the world, pretending to enjoy plays which their intellects have outgrown, and deafening their ears to the chatter of the young people, which under the most favorable circumstances must grow tedious often. Oh, the poor chaperone! It is the worst possible manners not to be gratefully attentive to her. It is also unrefined and indeed it would be selfish on her part, if she insisted upon attentions that were needless, or compelled the conversation of her charges to drift into currents that interested herself more than it could more youthful persons.

To be amiable and discreet, and to manage her charges in a manner to give them the most satisfaction at the moment, and also in memory, and to use as much courtesy and as little candor as is consistent with her duty, completes the chaperone's social mission. To earn for herself no greater aversion than is included in a general condemnation of her office is all she can hope for in this generation. The next cycle will know no other than the duenna and will be more just. Since the Atlantic Ocean has become only a short ferry, and social interchanges and family connections across it have become so common, we cannot afford to allow foreigners to suspect that our young women are not as tenderly prized and as perfectly protected as their own, and quite beyond the slightest danger of being held in disrespect. It was our relation to foreign society that compelled the introduction of chaperones and not because there was doubt of the honor of the American gentleman or the ability of a young American gentlewoman to take perfect care of herself.

It is bad form not to lift the hat when passing women in hotel halls, or when entering hotel parlors or waiting rooms where there are women; as an acceptance of thanks for assistance, or any courtesy that a stranger may offer; also in response to salutations made to those with whom a man is walking or in whose company he is; or at any place or time at which custom makes this easy mark of gentlemanliness and civility appropriate. To raise the hat when passing wherever the dead are being carried out is obligatory. It is an impulse with men of quick sympathies, and those who have little regard for the griefs of others will assume at least an outward manner of tenderness for suffering humanity. A man who fails in this mark of sympathy must be hard hearted, or very unpolished in manner.

Frenchmen in their own country uncover their heads while funerals are passing, and perhaps this is none too marked an expression of compassion, but such an extreme expression of respect is not expected in this country in the streets.

When a friend passes away, of course a note of condolence is written to the person most bereaved, and cards are left for other near relatives. This is done at once, and no response is anticipated, although, if the letter included inquiries, its recipients or another member of the household may answer. If no reply is returned, consideration for the sorrowing pardons the omission, and the silence of distressed persons is never considered bad form.

When a man resigns his seat to a woman, it is very bad manners if her escort also seats himself, while the person who was generous, or perhaps only self-respecting, is still standing. It is a lack of delicacy or fine breeding, or both, if the woman who has gained a seat by another's kindness does not thank him by words or by a bow, even though her attendant has done the same. We do not mean to say that such is the custom of New York women, but it should be.

No man, if he be not aged or an invalid, occupies a seat while any guest, matron, or even a young woman, is standing at a private reception. Of course, in public conveyances it is more chivalric, but it is not obligatory upon men to rise and give their places to women who are not elderly, nor noticeably feeble in health, nor have infants in their arms. The young and strong woman has no right to expect such kindnesses from men worn out by a hard day's work. Men have claims to as much comfort as they have paid for.

At nightfall, it is especially cruel, and indeed it is vulgar, for a woman who, being out because it suits her pleasure, gazes at tired men with an expression that says, " If you were gentlemen, you would rise at once."

There is a sort of woman whose eyes and manner inform such as fail to discommode themselves in her interest, that she looks upon them as brutes. Such a woman would unsettle, if any one could, the respect felt for womanliness. Happily nothing wears out the true man's inbred refinement of feeling, or lowers his standards of manliness. The duty he owes to himself and to society is always a respected obligation.

Then there are women who decline offers of seats, feeling sure that they are themselves less wearied than courteous men who rise for them. Men are sometimes offended if their offers of their seats are politely declined. Such resentment is without justification. No woman declines a courtesy as a courtesy. She is often aware that a sacrifice is offered to her, but being strong she is unwilling to accept a needless convenience at the cost of another's discomfort. Her delicacy should be respected. A woman of good perception sees or knows instinctively whether she will give more pain than satisfaction by declining a man's offer of his seat.

ENTERTAINING.

THE ostensible purpose of party giving is to provide pleasure for one's acquaintances, and to make any person uncomfortable, when avoidable, is bad manners. A crush of guests, therefore, is very bad manners. The best society resents a crush. It is foolish, indeed it is underbred, to invite a larger number of persons to be one's guests than can possibly be entertained properly. A lavish supply of wines and a costly supper do not compensate visitors for bad air and being compelled to stand for hours in a crowd, and this too for no reason in particular, except the fact of being upon the hostess's visiting list. A munificent feast fails to restore wasted energies, or tranquillize nerves that have been irritated by the annoyances of a crush, that cannot, in truth, be called good society, because such gatherings lack an essential elegance, without which social life is neither useful nor agreeable.

A clever man styled a crush "Human Herding." He did not mean to be discourteous to a host who suspected that he was not enjoying himself in his crowded house while clinging to a door ; he only intended to be descriptive, and he was. He was not that cynical person who said :

"Afternoon crushes with tea and wafers are the least expensive of all gatherings that have been devised for making a crowd miserable."

While enduring the miseries of a stand-up crush, he formulated, quite involuntarily, for he was not by impulse a reformer, an angry, or at least resentful epigram, that stands in many memories a forcible, correcting element. It is a stinging protest against the cruel, bad form of a class of entertainers that are happily on the wane.

Society means conversation—an interchange of accumulated and digested, and perhaps undigested, information. Of course, rational conversation at a crush is an impossibility. But as has been said, this custom happily is falling into disuse in the best society, dropping away with other bad manners. The woman who really entertains, limits the number of her guests to the room she has for them, always remembering that wit, humor, brilliancy, and even amiability, are not evoked in confined spaces. Ill-humor and general silliness thrive vigorously wherever guests find themselves subjected to annoying, personal discomfort.

Interchanges of speech in a crowded drawing-room cannot be dignified by the name of conversation.

A recent brilliant writer, upon the art of conversation, divides it into trivial and personal, which he says is characteristic of bad air and controversial brilliancy, which is at its best in groups that are so small that each guest may take part in it as either talkers or listeners.

Interchange of thoughts is or may be the most charming, as it is the chief element in social gatherings, and this pleasure is wholly impossible in crowded drawing-rooms.   There are persons who do not dance, others do not care for games in which skill is essential, and still others who cannot learn to talk well.   Alas! there are some most worthy persons, also, who are able to do none of these things; but they can be gracious in manner, and also considerately appreciative and commendatory of the gifts or attainments of others, and above all, they may be the most inspiring or attentive of listeners.

No one is able to set a standard for social acceptability, after having drawn the moral line, and also that essentially strict one of good manners—but perhaps good manners is morality.   Such as conform to the demands of etiquette certainly have kindly hearts, are truthful, respect and practise proper courtesies, and are surely able to give and to receive pleasure in society.   If they neither gain nor provide the highest there may be in life, they are far from being ciphers in its best elements.   A little mental energy might enlarge, in a wonderful degree, their faculties and talents for giving and receiving.

GOOD AND BAD MANNERS IN CONVERSA-TION.

UNFORTUNATELY, it is sometimes the man "who don't know that he don't know," who is most insistent upon being listened to. This fault is not confined to men, however. It is the ignorant who are inhospitable to another's opinions. Entertaining alien views long enough to judge them fairly is not adopting them, any more than it is including a person in one's family to ask him to dinner. The scoffer at any seriously formulated judgment shows bad manners. Equally bad are the manners of the endless talker, who, when he seems to have reached a place where a period ought to be placed, begins to talk louder and faster if any one tries to interrupt him. Another bad mannered person is the one who boldly or baldly contradicts. Dissent is allowable if cautiously expressed, but denial or contempt is bad form. Those who differ from each other in opinions, are in very bad form if they cannot meet in society and find harmonious topics upon which to speak to each other.

There is a kind of woman who is the *pétroleuse* of

society—she corresponds to the social anarchist—and who throws bombs of dissension into illy assorted groups, for the pleasure of listening and gloating over their dissensions. Such persons as cannot be peaceably inclined are not welcome in good society. They are justly shunned whenever they slip into it through an unguarded portal. There must be differences of opinion, and one conviction is as much entitled to kindly treatment as another, each person reserving to himself the right to preserve his own, but not to set it up in an antagonistic spirit, while at social gatherings.

Those persons who are able to be patient and sweet, and long suffering, under the infliction of the bore who is astride an uninteresting hobby,—a talking specialist who has not been invited to explain his views, a woman with the only baby she was ever interested in, the story teller who wishes to be conscientiously exact about the day and hour of an insignificant occurrence, and is running on and on, while an alluring talker is within speaking distance, should inherit the earth, also the heavens, for they are earning both. Such disagreeable persons are grievous blots upon the best society, and they cannot be excluded often, because they are set in the midst of charming family circles, whose feelings must not be wounded by a slight to any of their members. In their cases, however, perhaps because accustomed to such prattle at the fireside, patience has become habitual, and therefore easier to practise than the unfamiliar find it.

It is unfortunate that moral worth should so often be attended by talents for being stupid. Fastidious tastes and gifted minds have much to discipline them, even in the most exclusive circles, because women and men, greatly their intellectual inferiors, are often thrust upon them in a way that cannot be avoided. Society has no courteous method for relieving itself of its barnacles; would that it had! but he and she who are most beautiful in manner, accept their share of these social ills with a smile of toleration. Theirs is the flower of good breeding.

To converse is to interchange thoughts. To talk is, as a rule, to give opinions and experiences without expecting, much less desiring, to know anything about those of another. Talkers are to be avoided.

It is said that since general introductions have become less common in society, conversation has languished. This need not be true. Indeed, it is not true of those who are familiar with the best usages in cultivated circles. As was said in another chapter, a mutual acceptance of a common hospitality is an introduction limited only to the hours spent together under the same roof. The names of the different guests are unimportant.

Those who do not talk together at receptions may miss a golden opportunity that can never occur again, and besides it is discourteous to be silent and apparently uninterested in any guest one has voluntarily met. Beyond the pleasure of talking *incognito*, as it

were, and the satisfaction of aiding a hostess in making the evening delightfully social, it is an occasion
when personalities are impossible themes. The unknown can neither speak of themselves, nor of another,
unless it be a public character, but there are endless
subjects that are deeply interesting to cultivated people,
and timely topics that may be discussed entertainingly.
It is between strangers, who are wholly uninfluenced
by a knowledge of each other's social affairs, that the
truth is often most highly developed.

When society becomes adjusted to higher breeding,
conversation between unknown persons, who meet at
the bidding of a common friend, will be universal
here, as it is, and for many a year has been, in the
highest circles of France. Individuals will then be
able to choose each for himself and herself whom they
will know afterward—if both are agreed—and it will
be a distinct gain for society.

Among people known to each other, thoughtfulness
in selecting subjects for conversation that have no
pain in them for others, is not as widely recognized a
virtue as it should be. Of course, a guest cannot
always know the fads and follies, the sweet and bitter,
of those with whom he finds himself a comparative
stranger. Therefore it is bad form for him to lead in
a discussion, or to introduce any topic, such initiative
being the duty of the hostess or host, if it be not left
to one who knows the group, at least in a general
way.

IMPERSONAL SPEECH.

To speak with blame of any acquaintance is bad form in society, as it is in the worst possible taste to criticise ill-naturedly our political rulers. We may object to giving an important office to one whom we cannot respect, but after the voice of the people has set him above us, good manners command us to be silent. "Thou shalt speak no evil of the rulers of thy people" is one of the earliest of statutes. To obey is to set an example of regard for the highest authority we know, and of veneration for those precepts, which, when obeyed, produce harmony at home and in society. Social conditions and aspirations, political and religious economics, literature and literary men, music and musicians, art and artists, mechanism and mechanics, science and scientists—indeed, almost everything interesting is within the limits of fitting conversation. We should not discuss, however, the private affairs of mutual acquaintances, unless it is done in a brief and casual manner, to applaud or to rejoice over them. Nothing is so lowering to social and individual tone as critical gossip as to

35.

personal and small affairs, and nothing so clearly and quickly reveals the grade of another's breeding to one who has been educated to feel a proper dislike and contempt for talk of this nature.

THE VOICE.

A CLOSE observer wrote long ago that a sweet conversational voice testified to a strain of good blood in the speaker's ancestry, no matter how squalid his own birth may have been.

This may have been true when it was written, but it is doubtful if any voice is so disagreeable in this era that it cannot be trained to sweetness or at least to an agreeable tone and modulation, unless disease or age has ruined the vocal organs.

In educated circles, a harsh voice is not so uncommon as it is a needless blemish. Correct pronunciation, and alas! correct modulation, too, are not always among the charms of the learned, but they surely are characteristic of the well bred.

An agreeable speaking voice, and a correct articulation and pronunciation are among the early acquired graces of well born and carefully trained children. Whining, nasal and thin, high-pitched voices are physical misfortunes to which medical, hygenic, and gymnastic remedies are now skilfully, and satisfactorily applied. " It was not so much what she said as how

she said it, that told me she was a gentlewoman,"
explained Washington Irving, when describing his
first interview with one who afterward remained his
grateful friend and admirer.

Loud voices are offensive when volume of sound
is not required, also thin voices, when a chest tone
would enrich speech; and nasal voices, when
strengthening the vocal chords by persistently breath-
ing through the nostrils instead of the mouth, would
correct these evidences of an early indifference to
refined standards of speech. Uncultured voices, even
when natural sweetness has been denied, are now so
needless that it is bad form to possess them. Especially is a low, pleasant voice with perfect intonations
and articulations a recommendation to good society.
An uncontrolled voice is a brutal offence and wholly
unpardonable.

There was a time when profanity was neither inele-
gant nor especially sinful, and he who could pro-
nounce oaths with what was then considered elegance
and facility, or had a gift of originality in epithets and
exclamations, was admired by his fellows. Even some
women of rank were said to cultivate the art. This
phase of coarseness existed in society a century or so
ago. The most that has been written or said in its
favor within the last score of years is: "There is no
elegance in profanity, but it does lend emphasis to a
sentence." We have reached that grade of refinement, however, when emphasis is not agreeable; the

truth, tranquilly told, impresses its hearers more profoundly than when it is spoken boisterously and with an accentuation that is more a matter of temperament or disturbed nerve centres than of intellectual fervor.

Profanity has become intolerable. Indeed, it is never used by refined persons, or by those who claim a place, or even a recognition in good society.

Slang is epigrammatic. Sometimes it is picturesque or very droll, but like a stranger, who brings no proper or trustworthy introduction, it is not welcomed in refined circles, and gains no place in pure English until it has a printed definition in a respected lexicon, after which courageous persons introduce it into common use. The stranger also receives recognition, after he has been certified.

Fastidious tastes are offended with slang; therefore as long as a word has not the stamp of scholarly approval, it is bad form to be familiar with it in society. If it is used at home, it will unexpectedly appear in public to the chagrin of its forgetful custodians.

GESTURE.

COMPOSURE is good form. Tranquillity is self-mastery, and therefore a part of culture or breeding. An active use of the hands while talking is unpleasant to everyone but the speaker, who as a rule appears to find much gratification in an exercise that belongs by approval to the orator or the actor.

In the days of political intolerance in France, where the opinions of men and women were in danger of leading them to the guillotine, gesticulation was used to take the place of speech, or rather to conceal an utterance. No one could testify in court to the meaning of a gesture, although its significance was seldom misunderstood. Of the remnants of this mode of communication, the shrug, the most offensive of gestures, remains in use by thoughtless, or vicious persons. It is, however, in the worst possible form. It may be made to signify or to suggest anything.

A shrug is not unlike an anonymous letter of detraction, or accusation, which the author is too cowardly to father openly. The shrug may mean contempt, open contradiction, or anything and every-

40

thing that is unpleasant and likely to be unjust, but in any event so uncandid an accusation must be looked upon with suspicion. No one shrugs his shoulders to convey a good impression.

Shrugs have no place among refined personal habits or elegant social customs. Nor can we welcome it among the many charming French usages that have been added to our social customs and personal graces.

VISITS OF FRIENDSHIP AND CEREMONY.

YOUNG married, and unmarried men call upon the women of the visiting circles of their families at least once a year, even when they have no party visits of ceremony to live up to, the latter being imperative social duties, in addition to annual calls. Older men who have wives or daughters are allowed to delegate this service to them.

Young men who wish to be included in a season's round of dances, dinners and receptions, cannot expect to be asked unless their cards, with their addresses upon them, are left upon their friends and acquaintances early in the season. (See " Good Form in Cards.")

They may or may not be received thus early, but calls of inquiry are expected. Ladies who are not at home to visitors until after a general reception, or at least not until they have sent out at-home cards, are allowed by custom to deny themselves to all casual callers. When they do admit a visitor at so early a time, it is a mark of especial courtesy.

Young women who have been in society two seasons, also young matrons, may make ceremonious calls, and pay visits for their elders during the early part of a social season, except when a stranger in town is to be given a dinner, in which case no one less important than the hostess herself—unless she is an invalid—can properly perform this courtesy.

The man caller leaves his overcoat, umbrella and overshoes in the hall, etiquette allowing him if he chooses to carry his hat and cane into the drawing-room, when his visit is made by daylight, unless it is during a special afternoon reception when he should leave them in the dressing-room. He may hold his hat and cane in one hand or deposit them beside his chair during a visit. If his call is to be very brief, he is sure to retain them in his hand while he remains in the drawing-room, and he need not be seated if he prefers to stand. It goes without saying that no man who is a gentleman, or hopes to be considered one, will sit while any woman is standing in a drawing-room unless he is an invalid or is aged.

For a man to maintain an easy and elegant standing posture is to have acquired an unconsciousness of self while in society, and at the same time to be able to express an appreciation of the honor and the pleasure of being included in the favored circle which his hostess adorns. His deferential manner, rather than explicit language, conveys thus much respect for her, and incidentally of course for his fellow guests. Less than an implied respect would be ungallant. If such expression is insincere, all the worse for his own character, because sincerity only should prompt a man or woman to make voluntary visits, there being sometimes involuntary ones of ceremony after an extended and unaccepted hospitality.

It is a dull, indeed stupid hostess, or one who has learned little of the world in which she is trying to take part, if she does not distinguish between an empty compliment and genuine respect.

A hostess receives young men, who come in during an ordinary afternoon at home, without rising from her chair. She rises to greet elderly men. As a rule she does not offer her hand to men callers, and of course they cannot claim this privilege. If she is thoughtful and kindly, however, she extends her hand to such men as have passed that age when modernizing social customs is easy for them.

Young women of course rise to greet those men and women who are unmistakably their seniors, but the same respectful attitude is not taken when greeting young men visitors. Hand-shaking as a rule is in disuse, having drifted away from society along with many others burdensome customs.

Gloves of visitors are not removed during calls by day or evening. At ordinary "at-homes," it is optional with the hostess to wear or not to wear gloves, good form having set no mark of approval or disapproval upon their use at unceremonious receptions. At formal at-homes or afternoon teas, they are always worn except by such as sit by the tea urn.

The young man, who hopes to be of service to his hostess by carrying a cup of tea to a guest or returning an empty one, does not bring an interfering hat into her dining-room, when calling, but he still wears gloves. He need not know the persons to whom he conveys his hostess's simple hospitality, but he may, and should address them.

Unless he is thus occupied, he may leave at the entrance of other guests, bowing to his hostess first, and then to each one of her family, and last to the guests in general, provided the circle is not a large one or too widely distributed in the room for this civility to be recognized. If his hostess maintains the old, cordial fashion of hand-shaking and he has thus greeted herself and daughters on entering, he need not expect this on going out, nor is it good form that any one should attend him to the door of the receiving room. The formal custom of bidding or pressing guests to call again whether man or woman, is now in disuse. It is understood that calls are expected after one invitation or permission, either verbal or by card, has been given.

Calls should not be extended beyond fifteen minutes unless the guest is assisting with the tea. In a crowded room a briefer call is advisable. All that is appropriate may be asked and said in a quarter of an hour, daytime visits being allowed or demanded only for the sake of kindly inquiry, congratulation or con-dolence for the family and the same with other guests quite incidentally. Calls are not suitable occasions for an interchange of grave or carefully formulated opin-ions, which, when broken up into casual sentences, are too often dignified by the name of conversations.

To be funny, or satirical, or personal or pedantic, while making brief afternoon visits, is in very bad taste, because it is pretentious and egotistical. The funny or droll man in society is not the elegant gentle-man. The man who attempts to be facetious at such times misses an opportunity for being appreciatively or duly admired, and is in as bad form as if a dress suit had been worn when only a morning coat or walking costume was admissible.

Dinner tables and *conversationes* are the places for wit, humor and brilliant talks, and general *bonhomie* between guests.

INTRODUCTIONS.

GUESTS are not introduced to each other in a formal manner unless there is a special reason for making them acquainted with each other. At a party, also at many houses during an ordinary afternoon at home, the servant who is waiting in the hall announces each guest by name as he or she enters the drawing-room. At the latter, especially if the group gathered is not large, the talk is often general and he or she who does not take part in it is considered unamiable, unintelligent, or unfamiliar with the rules of modern good form.

A common acquaintance of the hostess is considered to have had "a roof" introduction and that is limited only by the length of the occasion which brought her guests together. An after acquaintance is not expected by her. If she is well bred, she gracefully includes, in her conversation, the names of those who take part in whatever subject is mentioned.

Women sometimes make delightful acquaintance with each other by "natural selection," and so also do men, but not men with women, although they may talk together while calling upon a mutual friend.

The hostess does not, or need not, hold herself responsible for the likings and mislikings of her guests, or their continuance or discontinuance of such momentary acquaintance. She evades this by avoiding introductions, but she does afford her circle the most charming opportunities for establishing pleasant associations. Well-bred persons know how to continue an acquaintance thus casually commenced, provided there is a mutual liking.

These customs are perhaps hardly fair to the man. Of course he may speak to those who happen to be near him, which speaking by the way does not establish the slightest claim to future recognitions. His hostess may perhaps present him to a friend, but he has no right to ask it, nor to feel neglected, much less hurt, if it is not done. If his hostess introduces him, he may reasonably anticipate a continued permission to address his newly made acquaintance, but she is the one to first acknowledge the acquaintance by a bow or smile. In large circles one bow often obliterates the memory of another, while the personality may be pleasantly remembered.

"It is your face I have failed to recall, not yourself," explained a beautiful gentlewoman to a young man, who was a second time presented to her by a friend, after the poor fellow had suffered not a little by